Christmas in LIVERPOOL

Our story begins
up in the North Pole...

... where Santa's sleigh
had just touched down,
after delivering presents
to every village and town.

'Another Christmas done!'
said Santa, full of pride,
as he stepped inside his grotto,
feeling very warm inside.

The elves were busy cheering,
their night now complete,
their tools packed away,
so they could go get some sleep.

So, with a cocoa in hand
and his bed so very near,
Santa was also ready,
for his own rest and cheer.

But then... Oh no!
What could it be?
The head elf rushed in,
as worried as could be.

'Santa! Santa!
a problem, I fear!'
shouted his head elf
as he drew ever near.

Then he held up the list,
and oh what a twist...

For the city of Liverpool
had sadly been missed!

'Oh dear, oh dear!'
Santa gasped in fright.
'No gifts for them
on this very special night!'

If I don't do something now,
then oh what dismay,
there'll be no joy in Liverpool
come Christmas Day.

So, to the workshop they ran,
both Santa and elf,
seeking the bag
on the Liverpool shelf.

But that's how they'd missed it,
as the bag wasn't there,
and at this time of night,
all the shelves were now bare.

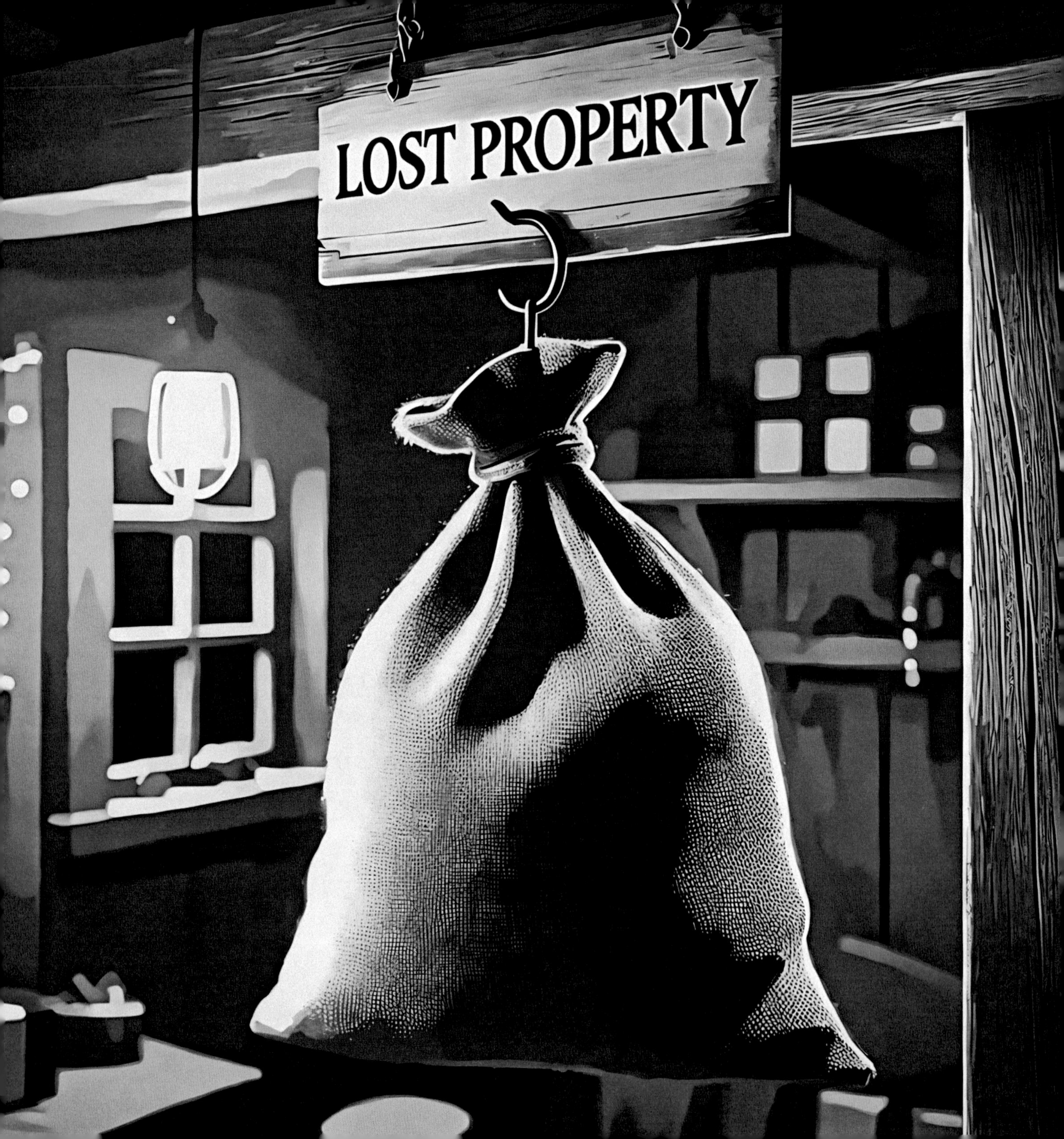
LOST PROPERTY

They asked all the elves,
and checked their log book,
then looked high and low,
inside every nook.

And they nearly gave up,
until one final look,
when somebody found it
on the lost property hook!

'We must be swift!'
Santa said with a cheer,
as he readied the sleigh
and gathered his gear.

The elf tossed the bag,
then the reindeer neighed,
and into the night,
their mission was laid.

When Santa finally arrived,
he smiled down at the sight –
of the lovely Liverpool,
all lit up at night!

The buildings rose so proud and tall,
in winter's gentle glow,
as Santa made his journey down
to the city streets below.

Next he flew to Albert Dock,
where ships were lined in rows.
then slipped down chimneys, one by one,
with gifts wrapped up in bows.

He left them snug beneath the trees,
all wrapped up on the floor,
then munched his way through all the treats,
until he could eat no more.

He soared above the museum's roof,
then over the Cavern Club,
to find each home upon his list,
and spread some Christmas love.

He flew by all the city's streets,
to every flat and house,
leaving gifts as people slept,
as quiet as a mouse.

Then he made some crucial stops,
amidst the busy city streets,
for all those huddled inside doorways,
trying to get some sleep.

He left some gifts by their side,
with a few extra to share,
so everyone could feel some warmth,
and know that someone cares.

Last he went to the student halls,
where lights were dim and low,
for any students still around,
as they couldn't travel home.

He left them gifts of warmth and cheer,
all wrapped in ribbons bright,
to lift their hearts and make them smile,
on lonely, wintry nights.

And so it was done,
his journey was through,
so Santa flew home
under skies bright and blue.

The reindeer were tired,
their work also done,
so they sped towards north,
till they reached morning sun.

But when he returned,
the silence was deep;
as the elves were in bed,
all lost in their sleep.

So he followed their lead,
and headed to bed,
keen for some rest,
for his now sleepy head.

'Merry Christmas to all,'
Santa whispered so light,
as he drifted to sleep,
after a very busy night.

He smiled as he dreamt,
all snug in his bed,
knowing the people of Liverpool
would feel warmth where he tread.

THE END

Christmas
in
LIVERPOOL

Made in the USA
Las Vegas, NV
12 December 2024

13999188R00026